CHINA

ISBN 13: 978-0-8249-6814-4 (softcover)
ISBN 13: 978-0-8249-6813-7 (hardcover)

Published by Williamson Books
An imprint of Ideals Publications
A Guideposts Company
Nashville, Tennessee
www.idealsbooks.com

Printed and bound in China

Library of Congress Cataloging-in-Publication Data

Florence, Debbi Michiko.
  China : with more than 40 hands-on activities to help experience China /
by Debbi Michiko Florence.
    p. cm.
  Includes bibliographical references index.
  ISBN 978-0-8249-6814-4 (softcover : alk. paper) -- ISBN 978-0-8249-6813-7 (hardcover : alk. paper)
  1. China--Juvenile literature. I. Title. II. Title: With more than 40 hands-on activities to help experience China.
  DS706.F6 2007
  951--dc22
                              2007038234

Project editor: Patricia A. Pingry
Book designer: Jenny Eber Hancock

10 9 8 7 6 5 4 3 2

Kaleidoscope Kids® is a registered trademark of Ideals Publications

Notice: The information contained in this book is true, complete, and accurate to the best of our knowledge. All recommendations and suggestions are made without any guarantees on the part of the author or Ideals Publications. The author and publisher disclaim all liability incurred in conjunction with the use of this information.

PHOTOGRAPHY CREDITS
Photographs on the pages indicated are used by permission:
Cover © Corbis/SuperStock; 9 © fStop/SuperStock; 10 © Michele Burgess/SuperStock; 11 © age fotostock/SuperStock; 13 © age fotostock/SuperStock; 14 © Photononstop/SuperStock; 15 © Kurt Scholz/SuperStock; 16 © Mick Roessler/SuperStock; 25 © age fotostock/SuperStock; 32 courtesy Debbi Michiko Florence; 33 courtesy Debbi Michiko Florence; 35 © Bridgeman Art Library, London/SuperStock; 44 © Mick Roessler/SuperStock; 46 courtesy Debbi Michiko Florence; 49 © Jon Arnold Images/SuperStock; 50 © Bridgeman Art Library, London/SuperStock; 57 © age fotostock/SuperStock; 58 © age fotostock/SuperStock; 61 © Steve Vidler/SuperStock; 62 © age fotostock/SuperStock; 64 © Christie's Images/SuperStock; 65 © Steve Vidler/SuperStock; 66 © age fotostock/SuperStock; 74 © SuperStock, Inc./SuperStock; 79 © age fotostock/SuperStock; 81 © Angelo Cavalli/SuperStock; 82 © Steve Vidler/SuperStock; 83 © age fotostock/SuperStock; 85 © age fotostock/SuperStock; 88 © Steve Vidler/SuperStock; 90 © Ron Reznick, www.digital-images.net; 92 © age fotostock/SuperStock.

To my husband, Bob, for the adventures in China—*Wo ai ni*.
—DMF

Thank you to my daughter, Caitlin Masako Schumacher for her help testing activities.
       Thanks to all my writer pals for support, particularly to Jo Knowles, Cindy Faughnan, Jo Whittemore, my awesome agent, Jennifer DeChiara, my fab editor, Pat Pingry, and most especially to Nancy Castaldo.
       Xie xie to the following people for information and assistance: Gail Hirokane, Lisa Fung, Niki Rein, Zhuang Cui Qing, Xin Hai, Scott Carter, Vivian Dong, Dai Zhiying, and my Mandarin teacher, Yang Lei.
       For love and encouragement, both sets of parents Bob and Yasuko Fordiani and Will and Nell Florence.

CHINA

OVER 40 ACTIVITIES TO EXPERIENCE CHINA— PAST AND PRESENT

Debbi Michiko Florence

Illustrations by Jim Caputo

williamsonbooks™
Nashville, Tennessee

SOME CHINESE SAYINGS

Reading without thinking will confuse you. Thinking without reading will place you in danger.

— CONFUCIUS

A clear conscience is the greatest armor.

—TRADITIONAL CHINESE PROVERB

One who sets his heart on doing good, will ever be free from evil.

—CONFUCIUS

To the good be good. To the bad be good, too, in order to make them good as well.

—LAO ZI

A bridge never crossed is a life never lived.

—TRADITIONAL CHINESE PROVERB

The enjoyment of food is one of the things that contributes to the peace and harmony of a society.

—CONFUCIUS

Make happy those who are near, and those who are far will come.

—TRADITIONAL CHINESE PROVERB

CONTENTS

Come with Me to China . . .

Imagine living in a country that has been around for over 4,000 years! A country where the mountains rise as high as the airplanes fly but also a country with a desert that is often covered with frost.

China is a country of contrasts and extremes and one with a lot of "firsts." It is different from us in just about every way. It has had and still has different forms of governments, many revolutions, interesting foods, and a unique way of writing. So we have a lot to learn when we take a look at China's past and present.

What will you find in this book? You'll discover China's long history. You'll speak Mandarin. You'll explore fascinating places like the Great Wall and Forbidden City. You'll learn about calligraphy and pandas and chopsticks. You'll cook dumplings, create clay soldiers, and play Chinese games. The following pages are just a glimpse into China; there's so much more to discover!

But before we dive in, here's a ditty I learned from my Mandarin teacher.

Zhong guo da,	China is big,
Ren kou duo,	Chinese people are many,
Fang yan duo,	Dialects are many,
Li shi chang.	History is long.

Now fasten your seatbelt, and come with me to China!

—*DMF*

China-A Country of Contrasts

About 1.3 billion people live in China and the country sprawls across 3.7 million square miles. In area, it is the third largest country in the world behind Russia and Canada. China's border touches three seas and fourteen other countries.

Say It!

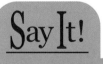

Zhong guo (jong gwoh) means middle country and is the short way of saying China.

7

A Contrast in States

C hina is not divided into states, but into twenty-two provinces (which are like states), five autonomous regions, four separate municipalities, and two "special administrative regions" (SAR). The autonomous regions are those areas where the population is not traditional Chinese, like Mongolia. Municipalities are some very large cities (like Shanghai), and the special administrative regions are Hong Kong and Macao, both once under foreign control.

Try It!

Can you locate the divisions of China, including the four municipalities and two special administrative regions?

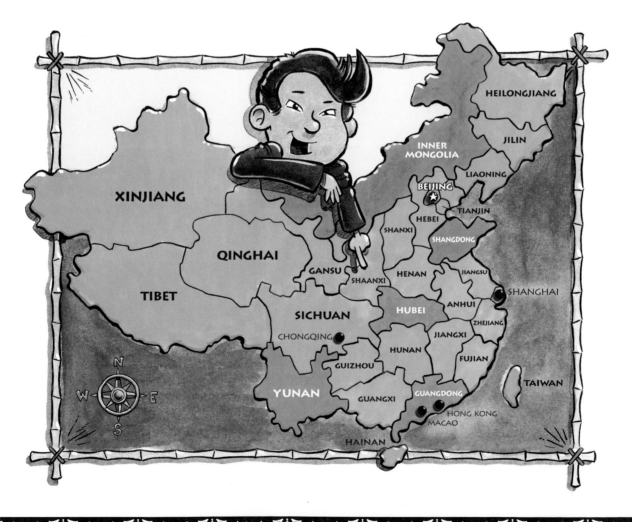

CONTRASTING GOVERNMENTS

Beginning in 221 BC, China was ruled by emperors and the rule passed to their children. Each family of rulers was called a "dynasty." When the ruling family changed, the name of the dynasty changed.

In 1912 peasants, led by Sun Yat-Sen, revolted and overthrew the last dynasty—the Qing dynasty. The peasants revolted again in 1949, this time led by Mao Zedong. After Mao took control, China became a Communist country.

SYMBOLIC FLAG

The flag for the People's Republic of China has a red background which symbolizes the Communist revolution. The large star stands for the Communist Party while the four smaller stars represent the people of China. The color yellow symbolizes China's bright future.

SO WHAT'S COMMUNISM?

Communism is a form of government in which everything is owned and controlled by the government. This theory of government was created by Karl Marx.

PONDER THIS

What is the form of government of the United States of America? How is this form of government different from China's government?

CONTRASTING CITIES

What's it like to live in China? If you were a Chinese kid, you might live in a huge, super-modern city like Shanghai with its noisy traffic, big ocean liners, and shops filled with everything you could possibly want. Or you might live in a small village with no running water, no TV, no shops, and where farmers still harvest grain by hand.

Say It!

Xiao Huang (she-ow hoo-ahng) means small and yellow.

Harvesting grain outside a small village

XIAO HUANG

In the Liping region is a small village called Xiao Huang. Only 700 people live here, and there are no shops or restaurants. The villagers grow their own crops and raise their own livestock for food. They even grow cotton, spin thread, and weave it into cloth which they then dye and make their clothes. There is no internet in this village. Imagine living without instant messaging!

A String of Pearls

It's hard to miss the Pearl Tower when looking at Shanghai's skyline. Rising 1,536 feet (468 m), the Pearl Tower is the tallest TV tower in Asia and the third tallest in the world. Visitors can ride an elevator to the top to take in the view of Shanghai. The Pearl Tower stands between the Nanpu and the Yangpu Bridges. The Chinese call the tower and bridges "two dragons playing with pearls."

Pearl Tower, Shanghai

Shanghai

Shanghai is the largest city in China. With a population estimated to be 20 million, Shanghai is one of the largest cities in the world. Shanghai was originally a fishing village.

Say It!

Shanghai (shahng-high) means "above sea" or roughly "city on the sea."

Ponder This

Landmarks make certain cities identifiable to people, like the Eiffel Tower in Paris or the Golden Gate Bridge in San Francisco. No matter how big or small the place where you live, your town has a landmark. Maybe it's a water tower or a historical house. What is your town's landmark? Make a list of other cities and their landmarks. Think about New York, Chicago, Seattle, Tokyo, London, and Rome. How many landmarks can you list?

Contrasting Environments

I f you lived in China, you might live on the island of Hong Kong or in the mountains within sight of Mount Everest or even beside the South China Sea. You might live in the vast, dry, but cold, Gobi Desert or on the plains of Mongolia. China is so huge that it covers many different ecosystems.

So What's a Bactrian Camel?

This is the camel with two humps. To remember this, draw a large capital B on its back. See the two humps? B is for Bactrian camel with two humps on its back.

The Gobi Desert

The Gobi Desert is Asia's largest desert covering 500,000 square miles (1,300,000 sq km). This desert sprawls from southern Mongolia into northern China. In China, it is called Gebi (guh-bee).

Temperatures range from -40°F (-40°C) in the winter with a little snowfall in some areas to 104°F (40°C) in the summer. Rainfall is usually less than eight to ten inches (20–25 cm). Since this desert is so huge, it shouldn't be a surprise to learn that the environment varies from waterless sandy areas to occasional shallow lakes and small creeks to thin growths of grass and shrubs.

You might think that no one could live in the Gobi Desert, but you would be wrong. Nomadic tribes in Mongolia make the desert their home. Many wildlife live there, too, like Bactrian camels, Przewalski's horses, the rare Gobi Desert bear, the Gobi wolf, and other animals.

Bactrian camels in the Gobi Desert

Try It!

Look at a globe and find the Gobi Desert. Now trace your finger to Beijing, and then to Shanghai, and to Korea, and, finally, to the United States. Sand from the Gobi Desert ends up in all those places. Almost a million tons of Gobi Desert dust blows into Beijing each year! Dust storms are sometimes so bad that people can barely see right in front of their faces. Sometimes people die during these storms.

PONDER THIS

Research Gobi Desert animals and try to figure out what adaptations help these animals survive in the harsh desert environment. Bactrian camels have large platter-sized hooves that keep them from sinking into sand, kind of like snowshoes. They also have long lashes and nostrils that close to keep sand out of their eyes and noses.

ON TOP OF THE WORLD

Mount Everest is the highest mountain in the world; it's 29,035 feet (8,850 km) high. That is as high as jet airplanes fly! Everest is in Tibet, a part of China. Known as Mount Chomolungma (Mother Goddess) in Tibetan, Mount Everest got the name we are most familiar with when a British surveyor-general for India named Sir George Everest recorded the location and height of this mountain in 1865.

Mount Everest is always capped with snow and covered by massive glaciers. This mountain is a mountaineer's ultimate climb. Since 1922 there have been over 180 deaths but mountain climbers continue to dream of reaching the summit of Mount Everest, truly the top of the world.

Mount Everest

PONDER THIS

Why do you think so many climbers risk injury or even death to climb Mount Everest? Think about some risks you want to take or have taken. How did you feel after you accomplished the task? How did you feel if you didn't succeed? Have you ever risked something that might cause you injury? Even some sports hold risks. Are the risks worth it to you?

CONTRASTING WATERWAYS

Say It!

Yangtze (yahng-zuh) is called *Chang Jiang* (chahng jee-ahng) by the Chinese and means "long river."

Huang He (huwang-huh) means "yellow river."

In ancient China, there were no highways or even narrow roads over most of its mountainous regions and rural land. The Yangtze River became a "super highway" across the country. The Yangtze is the longest river in Asia and the third longest in the world. It flows 3,964 miles (6,380 km) east across southern China, winding its way to the China Sea. Seven-hundred tributaries connect the river to small villages.

China's other long river, the Yellow River, starts high in the mountains of the north and meanders through the northern part of China. The Yellow River is the second largest river in China, flowing almost 3,400 miles (5,464 km). These two rivers provided watery "super highways" for ancient China and are important even today.

Wu Gorge of the Yangtze River

So What's a Tributary?

A tributary is a stream or creek that flows into a river.

RIVERS CONNECTING CHINA

In 486 BC, the emperor began digging a canal which would join the Yellow River in the north with the Yangtze River in the south. This canal would open up even more of China to commerce and communication, although the emperor really wanted the canal to better move his armies.

The Grand Canal, as it came to be known, at 1,100 miles (1,794 km), remains the longest canal in the world. This canal was originally dug by hand. It was completed during the Sui dynasty but renovated during later dynasties. For 2,400 years, barges and boats have used the canal to bring grain, coal, and other items from north to south and back again.

Try It!

If you have a river near you, do a little research. Where does your river lead? How long is it? Is it used mostly for recreation or commercial purposes? Spend some time sitting on the banks and watching the river. Are there a lot of boats? What kind? Do you see wildlife? Or are there mostly buildings? Do you see anyone fishing in the river?

The Grand Canal

Say It!

Sui (sway) is the dynasty that once again united China.

Try It!

Trace the route on the map below of the Yangtze, the Yellow River, and the Grand Canal. List the cities that might have relied on the rivers and canal for their food and communication. Which areas were probably flooded by the Yellow River and which by the Yangtze?

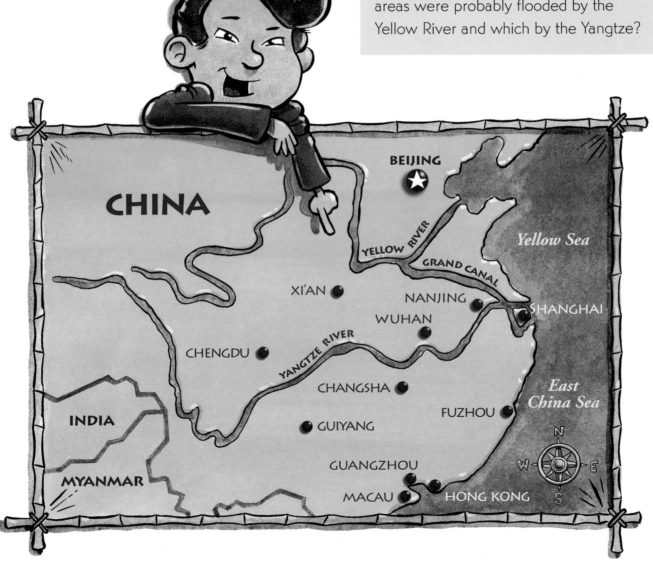

CONTRASTING OPINIONS

In 1995, construction began on the world's largest hydroelectric dam, called the Three Gorges Dam, on the Yangtze River near Yichang. The dam will be over 600 feet (182.9 m) high, 1.4 miles (2.3 km) long, and create a reservoir that will spread 350 miles (563.3 km) upstream. Sometimes people cannot agree on what is best for their country, and this is the case with the dam.

WHY THE DAM IS GOOD

The Yangtze River floods every year, damages houses and businesses, and kills many people. In 1954, the Yangtze flooded and killed over 30,000 people.

At present, the main source of energy in these areas is coal; but coal causes pollution and acid rain. The hydropower from the new dam will provide electric energy and reduce coal burning.

SO WHAT'S A RESERVOIR?

A reservoir is a lake that is formed when the dam blocks the water from moving downstream. This water is usually used as a source of water for a city or region.

WHY THE DAM IS BAD

Once the dam is operational, many villages, factories, and a lot of land will be underwater. People who live in those villages will lose their homes and their jobs. Cultural artifacts from thousands of years ago will be lost. Existing factories might contain chemicals that will pollute the water when they are flooded. Both farmland and wildlife will be lost to flooding.

HOLD A
TOWN MEETING

WHAT YOU NEED

10 or more people
Index cards

WHAT TO DO

1. Write each of the following on a separate index card. (If you have more than eleven people, then you can have more than one card with the same identity except for mayor.)

Mayor, fisherman, factory worker, worker hired to build the dam, villager, wildlife biologist, manager of the electrical plant, person who lost family in a flood, environmentalist concerned about water pollution, teacher, and farmer.

2. With the cards face down, have each person take a card. He or she acts out the part of the person on the card.

3. The mayor will call the town meeting to order. Pretend that a dam similar to the Three Gorges Dam is going to be built along a river near your town. You've read about the issue above. Depending on who your card says you are, argue for or against building the dam. Everyone gets a chance to speak and say why he or she is for or against.

4. After everyone has spoken, the mayor calls for a vote to see if the dam will be built.

A Superhighway across Ancient China

A ncient China also needed to ship goods over land, especially to the West. The Han dynasty built what came to be known as the Silk Road to move armies over land and for diplomatic missions to the West. Later, the Silk Road became an important trade route linking the Imperial Court of China to the Roman Empire. Bactrian camels, native to China, carried loads through the harsh conditions along the Silk Road.

The Silk Road not only connected China to the outside world, but connected Chinese cities inside the country, and it became key to providing information and news along the route. Think of the Silk Road as today's internet, except much slower and less technical.

As Smooth as Silk

Historians believe that the Chinese have been producing silk for more than 4,000 years! Silk production peaked during the Han dynasty (207 BC–AD 220) when silk goods were traded with other countries and cultures.

Ponder This

Can you think of any roadways in other parts of the world that link a country by road? Research the United States interstate system and Germany's Autobahn. Find out when these highway systems were built and why.

20

AN ANCIENT ROAD TO OTHER CIVILIZATIONS

The Silk Road began in Chang'an (the ancient name of Xian), reached the Yellow River at Lanzhou, then skirted westward along deserts and mountains before dividing into three routes at the oasis of Dunhuang. Ancient merchants and diplomats continued eastward until they arrived at Rome.

A ROAD BY ANY OTHER NAME

A nineteenth-century German scholar named this route "The Silk Road."

Contrasting Languages

People in China speak many dialects, although the official language of China is Mandarin. In Shanghai, residents speak Shanghainese or Mandarin, while residents of Hong Kong and Guangzhou mainly speak Cantonese. In this book, all Chinese words will be italicized and are in Mandarin, unless otherwise noted.

The Pinyin System

The Chinese use a system called *pinyin* with which they can write Chinese words with our alphabet. Pinyin letters are not always pronounced the same as we pronounce our letters. An x in pinyin sounds like *sh*. A q in pinyin sounds like *ch*. In this book, when there is a Chinese word, it is written in italics for pinyin and the pronunciation will follow. Ready to learn some Mandarin? Here we go!

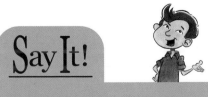

Say It!

Putonghua (poo-tohng-hooah) means the Mandarin language.

Are You Tone Deaf?

Each Chinese character has a unique sound. In addition to the sound, there are four tones for each sound. There is also a neutral tone. Depending on how you say it, *ma* could mean mother or horse. Imagine the trouble you could get into if you used the wrong tone!

For this book, we will ignore the tones; but, remember, that in Chinese the tones are important in conveying the exact meaning of a word.

HERE ARE SOME COMMON PHRASES AND WORDS YOU CAN LEARN.

ENGLISH	MANDARIN	PRONUNCIATION
Hello!	*Ni hao!*	(nee how)
Hello! (to an elder)	*Nin hao!*	(neen how)
How are you?	*Ni / Nin hao ma?*	(nee/neen how mah)
I am fine!	*Wo hen hao!*	(woh hen how)
Thank you.	*Xie xie.*	(she-eh she-eh)
Good-bye!	*Zai jian!*	(za-ee jee-ehn)
today	*jin tian*	(jeen tee-ehn)
tomorrow	*ming tian*	(meeng tee-ehn)
yesterday	*zuo tian*	(zwoh tee-ehn)
My name is . . .	*Wo jiao . . .*	(woh jee-ow . . .)

AND THIS IS HOW YOU COUNT TO 10 IN MANDARIN.

NUMBER	MANDARIN	PRONUNCIATION
1	*yi*	(ee)
2	*er*	(ar)
3	*san*	(sahn)
4	*si*	(suh)
5	*wu*	(woo)
6	*liu*	(lee-yoh)
7	*qi*	(chee)
8	*ba*	(baah)
9	*jiu*	(jee-yoh)
10	*shi*	(shuh)

Kids Will Be Kids!

Do you wonder what daily life and your school days would be like if you lived in China? Life in China is different depending upon whether you live in a village or a large city. You might be surprised to learn that school in China is not very different from yours. Chinese kids like to do many of the same things you like to do. But growing up in a country that is so ancient gives kids in China a unique appreciation of the past. Imagine studying 4,000 years of history!

LIFE FOR CHINESE KIDS

In the city, kids wear clothes similar to yours, like blue jeans and sneakers. There are department stores and malls, and kids ride on the backs of their parents' bikes between the cars, buses, taxis and motorbikes. In rural areas, people ride bicycles or walk. Kids might have to walk a long way just to get to a store. Some don't even have shoes to wear. Life in China is still a contrast from province to province and from a big city to a village.

SCHOOL DAYS

In China the first day of school is in September, and the kids go to school five days a week for nine months, just like you do. Students wear school uniforms until high school, where they wear the uniform only on certain days. There is a break for a week in October and a one-week spring break in May. Summer vacation is July and August. Does that sound familiar?

Children in China must attend school for at least nine years. Kids start primary school at about six years of age for six years; then it's on to primary middle school for three more years. School isn't completely free though. At primary school, Mom and Dad must pay a small fee for books, food, heating, and transportation. After primary school, students usually go on to secondary middle school (like your high school). There is a tuition charged for high school.

LEARN MORE·LEARN MORE·LEARN MORE·LEARN MORE·LEARN MORE·LEARN MORE·LEARN MORE·LEARN MORE

Would you like to read some picture books and novels about Chinese-Americans? Check out this great list of books (plus links to author sites) on Cynthia Leitich Smith's website http://www.cynthialeitichsmith.com/lit_resources/diversity/asian_am/chinese.html.

Street in Beijing, China

THREE DAYS IN JUNE

Students who want to go to college must pass *the* big test called *Gao Kao*. Test scores are so important because they will determine not only where the student can go to college, but even if the student will be allowed to attend college.

Gao Kao is given all over China on the same three days in June. Parents often travel with their children and wait outside the exam room as nervous as the students taking the test. Sometimes they hang banners outside that say "Keep Silent" so that noise from the street will not disturb the test takers.

KEEP SILENT

Say It!

Gao kao (gaow cow), means high school examination.

HOME SWEET HOME

In big cities, a child and his or her parents usually live in a small apartment. In more rural areas, however, houses are bigger and stand alone. Often the entire extended family with grandparents and sometimes other relatives live in the same house. Children often live with their parents until they get married.

HOMEWORK EVERY DAY

Children in China, particularly in the big cities, play video games, have computers, and watch TV; but parents closely monitor their children's free time. Education has always been respected in China, and today is no different. Weekends and other free times are devoted to doing schoolwork. If they can afford it, parents enroll their children in after-school and weekend courses, such as music, math, writing, and painting. When they are not studying or attending classes, children spend much of their time with their families.

NO SIBLINGS HERE

In 1979, the population of China was growing faster than housing and food supplies, so China started a "One Child Policy." Married couples are allowed to have only one child. There are some exceptions to this rule, but there are severe penalties for couples who have more than one child. This policy has resulted in children with no brothers or sisters or even aunts, cousins, and uncles. Can you imagine having no siblings or cousins or aunts and uncles?

PONDER THIS

What do you think would be familiar about your life to a child in China? What do you think would be very different? Ask your parents or teachers about how their childhoods were the same and how they were different from yours.

HAVING FUN IN CHINA

What do kids in China do to have fun? They play many of the same kind of games as you probably do, like running races or playing tag and hide-and-seek. Some games played by Chinese kids are similar to the ones you play but with a little difference. Let's look at some of the games Chinese kids like to play. (Note: As with many games, there are lots of variations.) You can try to play some of these.

JUMPING ROOM

Jumping room is like hopscotch and is played by boys and girls. Children draw a grid of squares on the ground with chalk and follow a certain order to jumping in and out of the squares.

KICKING IT

Kicking it is like hacky sack where the player kick-bounces an object alone or with a group of others. The *jian zi* looks like a colorful version of a badminton shuttlecock. It has a weighted base with feathers of many colors decorating it. The player uses his or her feet to kick the *jian zi* in the air and continue kicking it to keep it from hitting the ground. A group of players can work together, kicking it back and forth.

Say It!

Jian zi (gee-ehn tze) is like a badminton shuttlecock.

tiao fangzi (tee-ow fahng tze) means jumping room.

CHINESE JUMP ROPE

Chinese jump rope is traditionally played only by girls. You can find Chinese jump ropes in toy stores. There are also books about it so you can learn how to play. Chinese jump rope is like a giant rubber band. Two people on the outside "hold" the rope in place with their feet. The band is actually wrapped around their ankles forming a rectangle. The jumper does a series of jumps and moves in the middle, using the elastic band.

DODGE THE BEANBAG

WHAT YOU NEED

Beanbags
4–6 kids

WHAT TO DO

Divide into two teams. One team forms a circle around the other team and tries to hit the others with a beanbag. When a person is hit by a beanbag, he or she is "out." The game continues until there is nobody left in the middle. Try playing this with your friends!

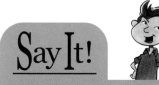

Say It!

Tiao pi jing (tee-ow pee jing) is the game of Chinese jump rope.

Da sha bao (dah shah bow) is the name for Dodge the Beanbag and means "hit the sandbag."

IT'S A SMALL WORLD AFTER ALL

Do you wonder what different kids in China like to do for fun? Here is how thirty-eight kids who live in Shanghai, and one boy who lives in Yuyao City in Zhejiang Province answer some questions about what they like to do. Write in your answer on the line provided. How different is your answer from the answers of the Chinese kids?

What is your favorite subject in school?

"Computing and English," Sen, age 16.

"Math," Zheng Yuan, age 10.

"English," Yu, age 7.

"P.E." Jie, age 10.

"Arts and crafts," Zhang, age 10.

My favorite school subject is _____

What do you like to do in your free time?

"Play the piano," Zheng Yuan, age 10.

"Read books," Sishi, age 10.

"Play football," Xin, age 10.

"Eat," Shengfeng, age 12.

"Watch TV," Si Qi, age 11.

In my free time, I like to _____

What is your favorite food?

"Ice cream," Yu, age 7.

"Bananas," Ru, age 11.

"Hamburgers," Pin, age 10.

"KFC," Yijie, age 11.

"Dumplings," Zheng Yuan, age 10.

"Chicken," Sen, age 16.

My favorite food is _____

What is your most favorite thing?

"Books," Yu, age 7.

"Soccer shoes," Sen, age 16.

"Hello Kitty doll," Xi, age 10.

"Beautiful doll," Wenying, age 11.

"Pencil box," Sheng Jie, age 12.

"Badminton racket," Ruchao, age 10.

My favorite thing is _____

What is your least favorite thing to do? Why?

"Play football. It is a boy's game," Lei, age 11.

"I don't like getting up. I'm very tired," Yueyan, age 11.

"I don't like cleaning my desk. It's big," Mengdie, age 11.

"I don't like climbing trees. It's dangerous," Shengquing, age 10.

"I don't like doing homework. It's difficult," Wenying, age 11.

My least favorite thing to do is _____

The Inventive Chinese

Many of the things we take for granted today were invented by the Chinese. Did you know that we can thank the Chinese for our fireworks? And for wheelbarrows, silk shirts, and beautiful porcelain? They also gave the world the compass, moveable rudders, and sails along with printing and paper. Where would we be today without the inventive Chinese?

SILK

Silk thread comes from the thread of cocoons produced by tiny silkworms, which are the larvae of the silkworm moth. Silk was so valued by the rest of the world that early traders from Europe smuggled silkworm eggs out of China and tried to introduce sericulture to Europe. Even in colonial America, some farmers in the southern United States tried to raise the silkworms.

One silkworm can make only about 3,000 feet (914.4 m) of silk thread during its short twenty-eight-day lifespan. It takes 111 cocoons to make enough silk for a man's tie and 630 cocoons to make enough silk for a woman's blouse. Because silk is so difficult to obtain, it is very expensive, even today.

Cocoons of the silkworm

PICKY EATERS

Silkworms are picky eaters. They will eat only mulberry leaves. After eating and molting, eating and molting, the silkworms spin a cocoon of silk. To harvest the silk, the cocoons are heated (which kills the silkworm inside). Then, the cocoons are put into hot water to find the loose end of the silk thread in order to unwind the silk. This is done by hand or machine. The raw silk thread is dyed and then woven into cloth.

FARMING WORMS

Sericulture, or silk culture, is the business of raising silkworms for their silk.

Machine unwinding silk thread from cocoons

LEARN MORE·LEARN MORE·LEARN MORE·LEARN MORE·LEARN MORE·LEARN MORE·LEARN MORE·LEARN MORE

Read the novel Project Mulberry by Newbery Award—winning author Linda Sue Park (http://www.lspark.com/books/mulberry.html). The main character is Korean-American, but the story involves raising silkworms.

FIREWORKS

Many of the things we take for granted today were invented by the Chinese. Probably one of the most well-known inventions by the Chinese is fireworks. Gunpowder, and thus firecrackers, was invented completely by accident. Around AD 700, alchemists were mixing different metals to try to create a potion that would keep a person alive forever. Instead, they invented gunpowder. At first the Chinese only used gunpowder for making fireworks; but by the tenth century, they figured out that gunpowder would make killing their enemies easier. So every Fourth of July, you can thank the inventive Chinese for your fireworks!

Say It!

Huo yao (who-oh yow) literally means flaming medicine and is what the Chinese call gunpowder.

Try It!

Do you think the wheelbarrow was an important invention? Test your theory with this exercise. Make a pile in your yard of at least twenty items (books, rocks, toys, things you can't carry all at once). Time how long it takes you to carry the pile by hand to another point in the yard. Now take a wagon or a wheelbarrow. Time how long it takes you to transport the same number of items back to the first point in the yard. Which one was faster? Which was easier?

WHEELBARROW

The Chinese invented the wheelbarrow during the Three Kingdoms dynasty (221 BC–AD 265). Wheelbarrows did not make it to the West for another 1,000 years.

CHINA TO EAT ON

We get our word "china," meaning the fancy dishes we eat on, from the popularity of the exquisite porcelain made by the Chinese and exported to the West. Rather than call the dishes "porcelain," the Westerners just called them "China" and the name stuck.

Porcelain is translucent (light will pass through it) but is very strong. True porcelain is made by firing a mixture of white Chinese clay (*kaolin*) and a type of stone (*petuntse*) to a temperature more than 1300°F.

Porcelain may date back to the Han dynasty, but true porcelain probably developed during the Tang dynasty. The most valuable antique porcelain, however, is from the Ming (1368–1644) and Qing (1644–1912) dynasties, particularly the blue and white porcelain.

The Chinese used the Silk Road to export their porcelain to the West, and it became one of the most sought after of Chinese inventions.

Blue and white porcelain from the Ming dynasty

Try It!

Create imitations of Chinese blue and white porcelain. Use clay and blue and white craft paint and see if you can create a miniature copy of a Ming bowl or vase.

WHEN CHINA RULED THE SEAS

During the Warring States period (403–221 BC), the Chinese invented a compass with a miniature spoon-type pointer. The compass pointed south and was used when practicing Feng Sui to figure out where to put buildings for harmonious balance with the environment.

During the Han dynasty (207 BC–AD 220), the Chinese invented a rudder for ships. The Chinese also invented sails that they could move. Before this invention, sails could not be moved so sailors had to wait for the wind to change. With movable sails, sailors moved the sail to catch the wind. With these inventions, Chinese ships could sail no matter which way the wind was blowing and, they could steer their ships.

By the time of the Song dynasty (AD 960–1279), the Chinese improved on the compass by using a magnetized needle that pointed north, and they used it on ships to help sailors navigate. With the compass that now pointed north, movable sails, and ship rudders, China ruled the seas.

South-pointing compass

SO WHAT'S A RUDDER?

A rudder is a flat piece of wood or metal near the stern of a ship by which the sailor steers a boat or a ship.

HOW DOES IT WORK?

A compass uses the earth's natural magnetic field with the "north" end of a compass needle pointing north.

MAKE A
COMPASS

WHAT YOU NEED

Magnet
Sewing needle

Facial tissue
Bowl of water

WHAT TO DO

1. Rub the magnet back and forth along the entire length of the needle (Fig. 1).

2. From one ply of tissue, tear a square just a little larger than the needle (Fig. 2).

3. Place the tissue on top of the water then put your needle on top of the tissue. The tissue will sink, but the needle will stay afloat (Fig. 3). You may need to poke the tissue with a pencil to sink it, but make sure you don't sink the needle. If you do, just start over from step 2.

4. The needle will spin until it points north (Fig. 4).

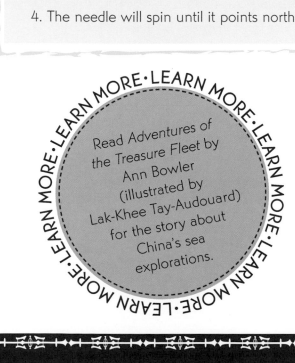

LEARN MORE·LEARN MORE·LEARN MORE·LEARN MORE·LEARN MORE·LEARN MORE·LEARN MORE

Read Adventures of the Treasure Fleet by Ann Bowler (illustrated by Lak-Khee Tay-Audouard) for the story about China's sea explorations.

Fig. 1

Fig. 2

Fig. 3

Fig. 4

THE INVENTIONS OF PAPER AND PRINTING

Where would we be without books? Before we had the computer and television, the only way people learned was through books. Even today, books remain a very important part of our lives. And what would you do without the library in your school? We can thank the Chinese for the inventions of paper and printing.

MOVABLE TYPE

In 1045, a man named Bi Sheng invented movable type. Characters were engraved onto wood blocks in reverse and then inked and pressed onto paper. This method didn't really take off in China because there were thousands of Chinese characters. In the fifteenth century, Johannes Gutenberg of Germany invented the printing press. Using twenty-six letters of the alphabet works much easier and faster, don't you think?

BOOK OF BONES

During the Shang dynasty (1766–1122 BC), Chinese people wrote on animal bones and tortoise shells. Later, they wrote on thin strips of bamboo.

BLOCK PRINTING

By the end of the Tang dynasty, the Chinese had invented a process by which they could engrave each book page onto a wood block and print books. This method was easier than individual moveable type. During the Five dynasties, bookshops were common throughout the cities.

PAPER

The Chinese tried making paper from hemp and silk waste, but none of these methods worked well. In AD 105 a man named Cai Lun invented a much improved version of paper. He mixed tree bark and bamboo fibers with water then strained the water out through a cloth.

MAKE YOUR OWN
PAPER

WHAT YOU NEED

6—8 pages of scrap paper
    (no tape or staples)
    torn into small pieces
3-gallon tub filled with
    warm water

Dishtowels
Wire clothes hanger
Knee-high stocking
Stapler
Electric blender

WHAT TO DO

1. Soak paper in water for at least four hours. Lay a dishtowel out on a flat surface.

2. Pull the hanger into a diamond shape. Stretch stocking over the wire and staple securely so it stays on the frame (Fig. 1).

Fig. 1

3. For this step, you'll need an adult to help. Fill a blender halfway with warm water. Add two handfuls of wet paper. Cover blender and blend on medium until you can no longer see bits of paper.

4. Clean out the large tub and pour the soupy paper mixture into it. Fill tub with warm water and use your hands to mix well.

5. Holding the wire frame flat, dip it into the water mixture and move it gently back and forth. The paper mixture will form on top. Keeping the frame flat, lift it out of the water. Let water drip off the bottom (Fig. 2).

Fig. 2

6. Flip your screen over and onto the dishtowel, paper-mixture side down. Gently press the stocking, pushing the paper onto the towel as you slowly lift the frame (Fig. 3).

7. Carefully pick up the paper and put it on a flat surface to dry overnight. The next morning you will have paper that you made yourself!

Note: Make several pieces of paper with the soupy mixture you have. If you throw away the leftovers, DO NOT wash them down the drain.

Fig. 3

Chinese Holidays

Families in China get together and have fun and feasts on holidays just as you do in your home. On the next few pages are some of the biggest holidays in the year. You'll find that Chinese holidays are based on a different calendar than ours in the West, and the events may seem unusual to you. You'll see that symbols are very important in these celebrations; and you might also see that luck is very important.

WHAT'S YOUR (CHINESE) SIGN?

FIND THE YEAR OF YOUR BIRTH, NOTE YOUR SIGN, AND READ THE DESCRIPTION ON THE NEXT PAGE. DOES THAT SOUND LIKE YOU?

1972, 1984, 1996, 2008 - Rat
1973, 1988, 1997, 2009 - Ox
1974, 1986, 1998, 2010 - Tiger
1975, 1987, 1999, 2011 - Rabbit
1976, 1988, 2000, 2012 - Dragon
1977, 1989, 2001, 2013 - Snake
1978, 1990, 2002, 2014 - Horse
1979, 1991, 2003, 2015 - Sheep
1980, 1992, 2004, 2016 - Monkey
1981, 1993, 2005, 2017 - Rooster
1982, 1994, 2006, 2018 - Dog
1983, 1995, 2007, 2019 - Boar/Pig

CHINESE NEW YEAR

Chinese New Year is the most important holiday in China; but it is not on January 1. The Chinese use a Lunar Calendar for holidays, based on the cycles of the moon. Chinese New Year dates change from year to year. The New Year is a spring celebration and a time for family reunions and visiting friends and relatives. The Chinese New Year celebration takes place over fifteen days and ends on the full moon.

During New Year, Chinese families set off lots of very loud firecrackers to drive away evil spirits.

PERSONALITIES OF PEOPLE BORN UNDER CHINESE ANIMAL SIGNS

RAT	OX	TIGER	RABBIT
curious, charming, generous, sometimes greedy, quick-tempered	patient, dependable, sometimes stubborn, judgmental	courageous, warm-hearted, sometimes moody, suspicious	shy, sentimental, sometimes secretive, negative
DRAGON	**SNAKE**	**HORSE**	**SHEEP**
smart, determined, sometimes demanding, stubborn	popular, hard-working, sometimes demanding, possessive	energetic, frugal, sometimes rebellious, impatient	artistic, imaginative, sometimes shy, nervous
MONKEY	**ROOSTER**	**DOG**	**BOAR OR PIG**
fun-loving, energetic, curious, sometimes selfish	honest, observant, sometimes argumentative	brave, loyal, sometimes stubborn, moody	honorable, courageous, sometimes stubborn

NEW YEAR TRADITIONS

Chinese families have many ancient traditions to observe during the long New Year celebration. One of the most unusual traditions is that everyone celebrates the same birthday! Luck is so important to the Chinese, that they do certain things to make sure they have good luck and no bad luck will come to them. Here are a few of the many Chinese New Year traditions.

FRESH START

The house is cleaned from top to bottom to prepare for a new year. It is very important to finish cleaning by New Year's Eve or the good luck might be accidentally swept out of the house!

KITCHEN GOD

The Chinese believe that the Kitchen God watches over their family. The week before New Year's Day, the Kitchen God reports to Heaven on the behavior of the family over the past year. Families try to get a favorable report by bidding him good-bye with a dinner of sweets and honey. Does the Kitchen God remind you a little of Santa Claus?

BIG FEAST

Cooking begins two days before the feast. All knives are put away before the New Year to avoid cutting the good luck. On the day of celebration, families share a huge meal. It's important to speak only positive words, because saying negative things on this day could bring bad luck.

GIFTS

Children receive little red envelopes called *hong bao* (or *lai see* in Cantonese) from relatives. What's inside the envelope? Money! It's considered polite to wait until the giver is gone before opening the envelope.

LIGHTS

The last day of the New Year celebration is on the first full moon of the Lunar year. It is called Lantern Day, and people light lanterns and hang them to welcome in the light of spring.

HAPPY BIRTHDAY!

Everyone turns a year older on the same day. Traditionally, the seventh day of the New Year is considered everyone's birthday.

LUCKY SIGNS

The Chinese hang up red banners with wishes for good fortune and happiness. Red is the color for fire, which Chinese believe is the life energy and considered good luck.

FIRECRACKERS

Chinese families set off lots of very loud firecrackers to drive away evil spirits. Would you like that?

Try It!

Many larger cities in the United States have Chinatowns. If you can, go to a Chinatown during Chinese New Year to see the festivities. Then create your own Chinese New Year celebration.

HAPPY BIRTHDAY EVERYONE!

Say It!

Guo nian hao (gwoh nee-ehn how) means Happy New Year in Mandarin.

Dragon Boat Festival

The Dragon Boat Festival marks the beginning of summer and is celebrated on the fifth day of the fifth month of the Lunar Calendar. Usually the date falls between late May and June.

Dragon Boats look like very long colorful canoes with the bow shaped like a dragon head. The boat can be between 40–100 feet (12.192 m–30.48 m) long and up to eighty rowers can fit in one boat. Rowers in the dragon boat race try to grab a flag at the end of the course.

Dragon Boat Legend

During the Warring States period (403–221 BC), one of the king's ministers, Qu Yuan (choo yoo-ehn), was loved by the people, but the king sent Qu Yuan away. He became a traveling poet. When the king was defeated in battle, Qu Yuan leaped into the Milou River. Fishermen rushed out in long boats to save him, but they could not. They threw *zongzi* (a type of food) into the water to lure the fish away from him. To commemorate the memory of Qu Yuan, the Chinese celebrate Dragon Boat Festival.

Dragon Boat Races, Stanley Beach, Hong Kong, China

Say It!

zongzi (zong-dzuh)

Zongzi

During the Dragon Boat Festival, families make and eat *zongzi* in memory of the poet Qu Yuan. This is sticky rice filled with fruit, beans, or meat, wrapped with bamboo leaves or reed leaves, and tied with strings. The little packet is then steamed.

HAVE A
DRAGON BOAT RACE

WHAT YOU NEED

At least 4 people
Markers or crayons
8 x 12-inch construction paper
Stapler
Bandanna or scarf

WHAT TO DO

For each dragon boat team of two or more people, construct a dragon head hat with two pieces of construction paper.

1. Break up into teams of two or more people. Each team should draw the two sides of a dragon's head on two pieces of construction paper (Fig. 1).

2. Staple the two pieces along three edges, leaving one long edge open to form a hat. Add decorations like glitter or streamers (Fig. 2).

3. Mark off the starting and finish lines. Place a flag (bandanna or scarf) at the finish line. Have a person named as a starter.

4. Each team holds onto the shoulders of the person in front. The first person wears the dragon hat. The more people you have on the team (in the boat), the more fun (Fig. 3).

5. Line up at the starting line and go! You can't run with everyone hanging on, but walk very fast. If someone lets go, start over. The winning team is the first to the finish line and grabs the flag.

Fig. 1

Fig. 2

Fig. 3

MOON FESTIVAL

The Moon Festival is a time for thanksgiving and usually falls between September and October. This festival began as a celebration of a good harvest; but today the celebration centers on giving thanks and reuniting with family. The round shape of the moon symbolizes the family circle.

The festival also honors the legend of the Moon Goddess. Families eat dinner outdoors under the moon to send good wishes to the Moon Goddess. They also eat moon cakes that symbolize long life and good health. Moon cakes are round pastries filled with sweet beans, dried fruit, or nuts. The center might have a duck egg yolk. If you find more than one yolk, you will have especially good luck.

SWEET INTRIGUE

A story goes that during the Yuan dynasty, the people plotted to overthrow their government. To spread the word, revolutionaries baked messages inside moon cakes and sent them out. The revolution was successful; the Yuan dynasty ended and the Ming dynasty begun. All because of moon cakes!

Try It!

Have your own moon festival by picnicking with your family under the moon.

Moon cakes

Real moon cakes take a lot of time and effort to make; but here is a recipe that is a simplified version of a moon cake recipe.

MOON CAKES

WHAT YOU NEED

An adult to help
Packaged biscuit mix
Ingredients listed on the package
Jam or jelly, peanut butter, pudding

WHAT TO DO

1. Preheat oven and follow the directions on package for mixing cut-out (not drop) biscuits.

2. Roll out the dough and use a round cutter to create moon-shaped biscuits. If you don't have a round cutter, use a small drinking glass dusted with flour.

3. Bake as directed on the package. Set aside to cool.

4. When biscuits are cool, use a blunt knife to cut a slit in each biscuit. Spoon in the filling of your choice.

5. Eat immediately! Yum!

Note: Once you fill the moon cakes, be sure to eat immediately. The moon cakes will get mushy and some fillings, like pudding, will spoil unless refrigerated.

Religion, Philosophy, AND Good Luck

Some religions and philosophies have been in China for centuries. Taoism and Buddhism are the two most prominent religions. Confucianism and Feng Shui are philosophies that have influenced the people of China. All four of these philosophies have influenced almost every part of everyday life in China.

TAOISM

Taoism was conceived by a man named Lao Zi, who was born in 604 BC. He believed that people should lead simple lives and not interrupt the balance of nature. What he called *yin* and *yang* are complementary forces like light and dark, hot and cold.

Yin-Yang

The Symbol of Taoism

LAO ZI SAID . . .

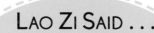

"Be a leader, not a master."

"He who knows others is learned; he who knows himself is wise."

WHAT DO TAOISTS BELIEVE?

• Tao is the origin of the Universe and the creator of all things but is not a god.

• Humans can achieve immortality by doing good deeds and reaching for moral integrity.

• Taoists follow the rules of nature instead of fighting nature.

• They adopt an attitude of "do nothing"; let nature govern.

• Taoists practice simplicity, compassion, and moderation.

BUDDHISM

Buddhism came to China from India during the Han dynasty and is based on the teachings of Siddhartha Gautama. Han (or Chinese) Buddhism is only one of several different types of Buddhism. There are many Buddhist temples and statues in China.

Sitting Maitreya Buddha, Hangzhou, China

BUDDHA SAID . . .

"It is better to travel well than to arrive."

"What we think, we become."

"A dog is not considered a good dog because he is a good barker.
A man is not considered a good man because he is a good talker."

RUB A BUDDHA BELLY

Lingying Buddhist Temple was founded by an Indian monk in AD 326. On the temple path are more than 300 Buddhist statues carved right into the rock. The most famous one is the Laughing Buddha. It is said that if you rub his belly, he can make your wishes come true.

WHAT DO BUDDHISTS BELIEVE?

- Reincarnation: After death, people come back to live again on earth.
- Middle Way: Life should be lived in moderation, neither in poverty nor luxury.
- Enlightenment: When a person achieves enlightenment (Nirvana), the cycle of reincarnation will be broken and he or she becomes free of all suffering.
- Equality: All living things are equal.
- Karma: Actions have consequences.

CONFUCIUS

Confucius is sometimes called the "uncrowned emperor of China" because he had such a big impact on the Chinese. Confucius was born Kong Fu-Zi in 551 BC during the Zhou dynasty. He believed in being kind to all, and he believed that everyone deserved an education and should learn to think and form their own opinions. His disciples wrote down his teachings in a book. After the death of Confucius, his students and disciples spread his word. Confucianism is considered a philosophy rather than a religion.

CONFUCIUS SAID . . .

"Forget injuries, never forget kindness."

"Reading without thinking will confuse you. Thinking without reading will place you in danger."

"When anger rises, think of the consequences."

WHAT DO CONFUCIUSISTS BELIEVE?

- They revere their family and parents.
- They believe in honesty.
- They revere loyalty to the state (government).
- They practice kindness toward others.

Confucius, 17th Century Chinese Art, Bibliotheque Nationale, Paris

FENG SHUI

Feng shui is the ancient philosophy of living in harmony with the natural world. Practitioners situate objects and even buildings for perfect balance and harmony. Emperors used *feng shui* to figure out where to build their palaces so they could have good fortune and not have their energy (or *qi*) interrupted.

It takes many years of study and practice to learn *feng shui*. Practitioners use a special compass and he or she must understand and use the five elements: wood, fire, earth, metal, and water. There are, however, some simple ways to integrate *feng shui* to create harmony in your life.

Say It!

Feng shui (fahng shway) literally means wind-water.

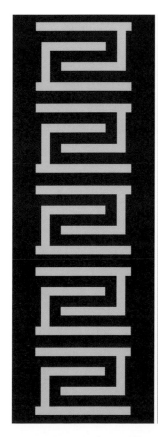

Feng Shui Your Room and Life through 5 Steps

1. *Positive Affirmations*—Focus on happy aspects of your life. Thinking negatively will focus on negative energy. Positive thinking focuses on positive energy. Try saying or thinking these things: "I feel happy." "I am healthy." "I did well on a test today." "I was nice to my friends."

2. *De-clutter*—Look around your room. If it is cluttered, the good energy might be blocked. This sounds like a sneaky ploy to get you to clean your room, but the *feng shui* truth is that a cluttered room can lead to a cluttered mind and unbalance.

3. *Money*—To increase your wealth, put a bowl filled with coins on a table.

4. *Color*—Wear pink to get rid of anger. Wear green for health. Wear yellow to help you study. Wear blue to have calm feelings.

5. *Better Sleep*—Make sure not to have anything stored under your bed or you may find yourself restless and unable to sleep.

China's Rulers

China's civilization reaches back over 4,000 years and is the oldest continuous civilization in the world. Until the twentieth century, China had the same form of central government that was set up by the first emperor.

You've probably figured out by now, that in China, history is identified by naming the dynasty under which an event occurred. A dynasty is the hereditary line of rulers, or emperors, and each dynasty contributed something unique. China still draws upon the traditions, arts, and beliefs begun in these ancient times. Let's take a quick look at each dynasty and what it contributed to China. A time line is on the opposite page to help you better understand the history of the dynasties.

Try It!

Make a time line of your life, starting with your birth. What are some important events in your life that you can include? Add world events that are meaningful to you. You can also include some photos of yourself on your timeline.

Xia Dynasty 2205–1776 bc

The Xia dynasty was long thought of as a Chinese myth, handed down through stories. But in 1959, scientists found proof of the Xia dynasty when they uncovered the Xia's possible capital. Historians, however, still don't consider the Xia a true dynasty.

SHANG DYNASTY 1766–1122 BC

The Shang is considered the first true dynasty of China. During this time, the Chinese developed a system of writing. People grew wheat and millet. Bronze was developed by mixing copper, tin, and lead.

ZHOU DYNASTY 1122–221 BC
- *Western Zhou 1122–771 BC* • *Eastern Zhou 771–221 BC*
- *Spring and Autumn 771–481 BC* • *Warring States 403–221 BC*

The Western and Eastern divisions of the Zhou dynasty marks where the capital was at the time. Beginning with the Zhou, the emperor was the authority between heaven and earth. A feudal system was introduced, meaning the land *and the people* belonged to the king! There were many wars. Confucianism and Taoism came into being.

Say It!

Xia (she-ah)

Shang (shahng)

Zhou (joh)

Qin (cheen)

Han (hahn)

QIN DYNASTY 221–207 BC

Shi Huangdi was the first emperor of China. He built roads, canals, a tomb, and the Great Wall. He standardized language, writing, measurements, and coins. But he also burned books and executed people who followed Confucianism.

HAN DYNASTY 207 BC–AD 220

The Han dynasty honored the teachings of Confucius. To work for the civil service system, a man had to pass a test on Confucian ideals. Han emperors built the Silk Road for diplomatic missions, invented paper, and created factories to manufacture plows and silk.

2205–1776 BC	Xia Dynasty
1766–1122 BC	Shang Dynasty
1122–221 BC	Zhou Dynasty
221–207 BC	Qin Dynasty
207 BC–AD 220	Han Dynasty
220–589	Three Kingdoms/ Period of Division
589–618	Sui Dynasty
618–907	Tang Dynasty
907–960	Five Dynasties
960–1279	Song Dynasty
1279–1368	Yuan Dynasty
1368–1644	Ming Dynasty
1644–1912	Qing Dynasty
1912–1949	Republic of China
1949–present	People's Republic of China

THREE KINGDOMS/PERIOD OF DIVISION AD 220–589

There were constant wars during this period. Buddhism spread and gunpowder was invented, although for many years it was used only for fireworks. For awhile, north and south China were separated into two countries.

SUI DYNASTY 589–618

The Sui dynasty again unified China and completed building the Grand Canal.

Say It!

Sui (sway)

Tang (tahng)

Yuan (ye-en)

Qing (ching), the last dynasty of China

TANG DYNASTY 618–907

The Tang dynasty set up a centralized government, in which the emperor was the final authority, and a legal system in which crimes were described along with the punishment for each. This Tang code still exists today. The government provided widespread education.

FIVE DYNASTIES AND TEN KINGDOMS PERIOD 907–960

China was divided (again) into north and south. The north was ruled by foreigners and always at war. The south was subdivided into ten separate states and grew culturally and economically.

SONG DYNASTY 960–1279

China was reunited (again!) and life was peaceful because the Song emperors just paid off their enemies! China's ships ruled the seas and her merchants traded all over the world. Education spread, printing improved, and books became available.

YUAN DYNASTY 1279–1368

Mongolian hordes led by Kublai Khan conquered China in 1279 and established the Yuan dynasty, the first foreign rule of all China. The Mongols spoke different languages, had different dress, and different customs. Chinese were not allowed to hold government positions. The first Europeans visited China during the Yuan (including the legendary Marco Polo) and international trade began.

MING DYNASTY, 1368–1644

Chinese peasants overthrew the Mongols; the Ming was the last dynasty with native Chinese in control. Chinese explorers sailed as far away as the east coast of Africa.

QING DYNASTY 1644–1912

During the Qing dynasty, Manchu, from the country of Manchuria, ruled the Chinese. The Qing made Chinese men shave their heads and wear *queues* and Manchu clothes. During early Qing rule, the country was prosperous in arts, culture, and trade. But later, China fell behind in technology and industry for the first time in history.

SO WHAT'S A QUEUE?

A *queue* is one long braid at the back of the head.

PONDER THIS

Can you name any other country that required certain people to wear something that set them apart from the others? Think about Nazi Germany.

REPUBLIC OF CHINA 1912–1949

In 1912 Sun Yat-Sen (Sun Yixian) led a revolution and established
the Republic of China. At the same time, a struggle began between
the Nationalist Party and the Chinese Communist Party (CCP). In
1926 Chiang-Kai Shek became the leader of the Nationalists and
Mao Zedong was gaining support as leader of the Communists. In
January 1949, the Communists took control of China without a
fight. Chiang-Kai Shek fled to Taiwan, an island off the coast of
China. On October 1, 1949, Mao Zedong established the People's
Republic of China with Beijing as its capital.

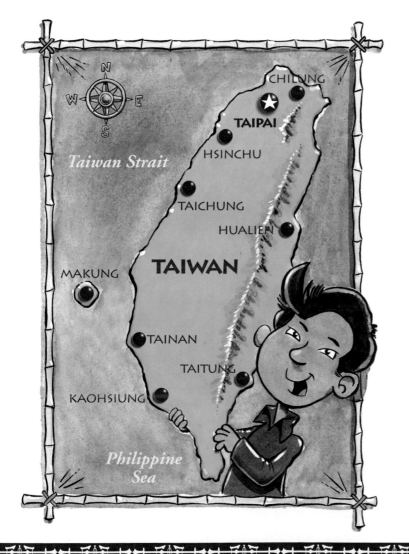

SO WHO OWNS TAIWAN?

China claims Taiwan as one of its
provinces, but Taiwan considers
itself an independent country.

PONDER THIS

Do you know when the American
Revolution began? Why did
Americans revolt? Who was
their leader? What was
the government after
the Revolution?

THE PEOPLE'S REPUBLIC OF CHINA

Mao Zedong became the leader of China in 1954. In 1958 he began a plan called "The Great Leap Forward" under which he created over 20,000 communes. The plan failed and many people died of starvation.

In 1966, Mao created The Great Proletarian Cultural Revolution. Millions of educated people were forced to work on farms to be "re-educated." Thousands of people were executed for having beliefs and ideas different from the government's. On September 9, 1976, Mao Zedong died and the era of modern China began.

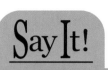

Say It!

Zhonghua Renmin Gonghe Guo (jong-hooah ren-meen gohng-huh gwoh) is Chinese for The People's Republic of China.

Portrait of Mao Zedong at the Gate of Heavenly Peace in Tiananmen Square, Beijing, China

CHINA TODAY

Since Mao's death, China has gradually become a modern world economy. The present leader is President Hu Jintao. China is still officially a Communist country.

Seeing the Past Today

Would you like to take a peek into China's past? China's history is long, but we can glimpse some of its past by taking a look at the remains still there today. We can even see China's army of 237 BC!

DIGGING AROUND IN THE PAST

On March 29, 1974, farmers discovered the tomb of the first emperor, Emperor Shi Huangdi. The emperor had the tomb built to guard him in the afterlife. He had a terra-cotta army made with warriors, horses, and carriages. The warriors and horses are lifesized and arranged in battle formation. Some archaeologists believe that each warrior was modeled after a real warrior since each face is different.

Emperor Shi Huangdi's Terra-cotta Warriors

So What's an Archaeologist?

An archeologist is a person who learns about historic and prehistoric people and cultures by studying artifacts and other remains left behind and which are dug up.

Fig. 1

Fig. 2

Fig. 3

Fig. 4

MAKE YOUR OWN
CLAY SOLDIERS

WHAT YOU NEED

Air-dry clay (available at craft stores)
Pencil
Craft paint

WHAT TO DO

The terra-cotta soldiers were three-dimensional, but you can create two-dimensional, or flat, soldiers.

1. Press some of the clay flat until it is about one-half inch thick and six inches long (Fig. 1).

2. With a sharp pencil, cut out the shape of a soldier. Make at least four soldiers (Fig. 2).

3. Let the soldiers dry according to the instructions (Fig. 3).

4. When the clay is dry, paint the soldiers. Make each one different (Fig. 4).

Note: Save for Try It! below.

Try It!

Think like an archeologist. Break one of your clay soldiers (but not in too many pieces). Keep track of the pieces. Using white glue and a toothpick (to dab on the glue), try piecing the soldier back together.

THINK LIKE AN
ARCHAEOLOGIST

WHAT YOU NEED

Several friends or family members
Shoebox or bag for each person

WHAT TO DO

Have each person take a shoebox home or someplace
where you can't watch them and place three or four
items in it that represent him or her. If he loves tennis, he
can place a tennis ball in his box. If she loves chocolate,
she can cut out a picture from a magazine or use an
actual candy wrapper and place it in the box. Make sure
the boxes have no names on them. When everyone has
finished, go through each box and try to identify which
box belongs to whom by using the items as clues. Were
you right? The better you know a person, the easier it
will be to figure out the correct answers.

THE GREAT WALL OF CHINA

Say It!

Chang cheng (chawng chuhng) means "long city." Over 4,000 miles (6,347 km) long, the Great Wall of China is truly a wonder!

The Great Wall is actually made up of many walls. During the Warring States period of the Zhou dynasty (403–221 BC) when China was made up of many different territories, each fighting wars with neighboring territories, rulers built walls for protection. When the first emperor of the Qin dynasty (221–207 BC) unified China, he also united the walls into one very long wall.

Try It!

How long is 4,000 miles? Have a grown-up set the car odometer to zero and drive one straight mile. Make note of the starting and stopping point. Now walk that mile. Imagine walking it 4,000 times and you have the general length of the Great Wall.

INCH BY INCH

For the original wall, workers first built up dirt. Then they built a wooden frame, filled it with loose dirt, and packed it solid. They added soil, layer by layer, tamping each down. The twenty-two-foot (6.7 m) high wall was literally built an inch at a time! Since then, it has been reinforced with bricks and stone. Many workers died during construction, and it is said that many were buried inside the wall.

The Great Wall of China

HALLS OF HARMONY

At the center of Beijing lies "The Forbidden City." This walled city was built by the third emperor of the Ming dynasty. He completed it in 1420. With 9,999 buildings, it is the largest palace complex in the world. This became home for the next 24 emperors and their families and the place where the emperor conducted state business. Why was it called the Forbidden City? The common Chinese person was forbidden to enter even the courtyard!

PONDER THIS

Beijing will be the site of the 2008 summer Olympic games. The emblem of the games will be a new Chinese Seal entitled "Dancing Beijing." The emblem symbolizes Beijing's hospitality and hopes and the city's commitment to the world.

There are also official mascots for the games. In fact, there are five of them. These are animals that are symbolic of China: the fish, *Beibei*; panda, *Jingjing*; the flame, *Huanhuan*; Tibetan antelope, *Yingying*; and swallow, *Nini*. When the Chinese names for these animals are combined, they spell *Bei Jing Huan Ying Ni*. This is Chinese for "Welcome to Beijing."

Even with the Olympics, the Chinese take their symbols seriously.

Outer courtyard of the Forbidden City

SYMBOLIC WATER

Yellow is the color of royalty and is used throughout the Forbidden City. The only building that doesn't have a yellow-tiled roof is the library. The Chinese believed black represented water and could put out fire. Therefore, the library's roof is black to protect all those books from fire!

THE LAST EMPEROR OF CHINA

The imperial family also had a summer retreat during the Qing Dynasty (1644–1912). There are over 3,000 structures in the Summer Palace. The Summer Palace is twelve-and-one-half miles (20 km) from the Forbidden City and a boat took the royal family to the retreat.

The Summer Palace was built between 1749 and 1764 and twice destroyed and rebuilt. This palace became the full-time home of the Empress Dowager Cixi, who spent a lot of the country's money rebuilding it. Empress Cixi influenced the government of China for over 50 years. She lived a life of intrigue and mystery!

Say It!

Cixi (tse-shee), the last Empress Dowager of China.

BEHIND THE BAMBOO SCREEN

Cixi became second wife to Emperor Wen Zong and bore him a son in 1856 who was the emperor's only male heir. After the emperor died in 1861, Cixi's son became the next emperor. He was only five years old! Cixi, the Empress Dowager, really ran the country. When the young emperor met with officials, Cixi sat behind a bamboo screen, listened to the conversations, then told her son what to do.

By managing the government, the Empress Dowager Cixi became powerful. After her son died at the age of nineteen, Cixi put her nephew on the throne. The day after her nephew died, Cixi died, but not before she put another emperor on the throne. He was three years old! This toddler became Emperor Puyi and was the last emperor of China.

China's Amazing Art

China's art covers many areas—from beautiful jade carvings to graceful calligraphy, and from restful music to energetic acrobatics. China's art is filled with symbols. Look for these in Chinese embroidery and jade carvings.

SYMBOLS FOR JADE CARVINGS

The Chinese often carve symbols from jade. For instance, a bottle stands for safety, a peach symbolizes longevity, a pair of ducks means love, and a fish symbolizes much money.

JADE

Jade is a hard, natural stone produced and mined in China. But to the Chinese, jade has almost mystical properties. Confucius said jade was strong like intelligence, had an internal radiance like faith, stood out like virtue, and was bright like heaven. To the Chinese, jade is a "living stone" and changes the more it is worn. The most common color of jade is green; but it is also found in shades of yellow, gray, black, orange, white, and lavender. Jade is often carved into shapes.

Carved green jade horse

A MYTHTERY

One day, Qian Long, the third emperor of the Qing dynasty, went to a lake for relaxation. He met and fell in love with a beautiful girl and spent a lot of time with her. Finally, his advisors said he must return home. The emperor was very sad to leave his love. He gave her a gift of a solid jade bangle to wear around her wrist.

Qian Long missed the girl so much that he sent his servants to find her and bring her to the palace. After searching for many days, they finally put signs up asking that the girl who received the jade bracelet from the emperor should step forward and receive life-long riches. To this day, girls wear jade bracelets in hopes of having a rich life.

SCULPT A
JADE FIGURE

WHAT YOU NEED

Colored soft clay that will air dry

WHAT TO DO

Take a large handful of colored clay and mold a figure such as a turtle, horse, duck, fish, peach, or bottle.

After you have the form just as you want it, set the clay aside to dry.

Jade bracelets of various colors

CHINESE WRITING

Chinese writing is in vertical columns and read from right column to left column, top to bottom. In modern Chinese, there are over 4,000 Chinese characters. Can you imagine if there were that many letters in our alphabet?

THE INVENTION OF WRITING

During the Qin dynasty, when the first emperor unified China, writing finally became standardized. Emperor Shi Huangdi created a type of writing that used 12,000 uniform characters called *xiaozhuan* (she-ow-jzuahn) or small seal script. The characters were used to identify ownership. The owner would have his name carved onto a seal, press the seal into red ink, and then stamp his seal onto official documents or paintings. Seals were made from bronze, jade, stone, and wood.

A seal made of jade

MAKE YOUR OWN
SEAL

WHAT YOU NEED

Scrap paper   Small knife   Paper plate
Marker   Small spoon   Small paint brush
Potato   Red craft paint   Construction paper

WHAT TO DO

1. Draw the first initial of your name on scrap paper with marker so that the ink seeps through the paper.

2. Flip the paper over to see the reverse image of your initial.

3. Ask an adult to cut the potato in half crosswise (Fig. 1).

Fig. 1

4. Copy the reverse image from your paper onto the potato half using the back of a spoon handle. Scrape away parts of the potato to make an impression of your initial. Be careful not to create any additional scratches or marks on the potato half. Make a small mark on the outside of the potato to indicate the top of the letter (Fig. 2).

Fig. 2

5. Squeeze a small amount of paint onto the paper plate. Use the paint brush to spread paint evenly so that you can press your potato seal into it.

6. Stamp the potato seal onto the paint, covering seal evenly but not too thickly (Fig. 3).

Fig. 3

7. Stamp seal right side up (the mark you made on the outside of the potato in step 4 should be facing away from you) onto construction paper. (Fig. 4)

Additional Activity: Using the other half of the potato, make a seal with the first initial of your last name.

Note: If your initials use any of the following letters, you can skip steps 1 and 2 since there is no reverse image: A, H, I, M, O, T, U, V, W, X, Y, Z

Fig. 4

THE FOUR TREASURES

The Chinese call the four items necessary to practice calligraphy "the four treasures." These are brush, ink stick, paper, and ink stone. Learning how to write and paint with these treasures takes a lot of patience, practice, and focus.

BRUSH

The artist uses different types and sizes of brushes to create different looks in the writing. The brush can be made from hair of rabbit, weasel, or horse. The shaft can be made from bamboo, ivory, jade, crystal, or porcelain. Beginners usually use a stiff brush since it is more difficult to use a soft brush.

INK STICK

When mixed with water, the ink stick forms the ink for writing. The ink stick was first made during the Han dynasty, with pine soot and glue. The ink was poured into molds and dried.

INK STONE

This stone has one end that is deeper than the other and is used for grinding the ink stick and mixing it with water to form the liquid ink. If the ink is too thick, the ink won't flow over the paper properly. If it's too thin, the ink will bleed all over the paper.

PAPER

Good calligraphy paper feels thin but is very strong because it's made of long fibers. The paper is very absorbent. If the calligrapher hesitates with his ink brush, a big blot will form.

CHINESE CALLIGRAPHY

WHAT YOU NEED

Pencil
Paper
Black craft paint

Round #6 paint brush
Small bowl
Small container of water

WHAT TO DO

1. Practice writing the Chinese characters that mean "mountain" and "center." Note the order of the strokes.

MOUNTAIN

CENTER

2. After you have practiced, try using your paint and brush to paint it.

3. Squeeze the paint into a small bowl and mix with water. The paint should not be too thick.

4. Sit up straight. Hold the brush upright and dip the brush in paint. Tap the brush on the edge of the bowl to get rid of excess paint. Draw the character large and in a smooth motion. Fill the whole page with the character.

If you'd like to try your hand at real Chinese calligraphy, you may be able to find Chinese calligraphy brushes and supplies at art stores or Chinese shops or online. There are books available that teach more about this ancient art.

Chinese 1 to 10

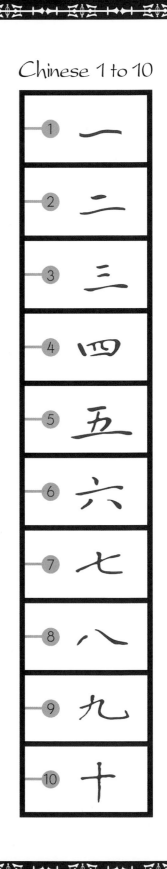

SYMBOLS FROM ANCIENT CHINA

China is a modern country, but ancient symbols are still very meaningful. Chinese writing began with symbols; and even today symbols are important, especially in Chinese art. Here are some of the symbols used most often in the daily life of China.

PHOENIX
The Chinese phoenix is considered the king of birds and represents virtue, grace, power, and wealth. It became the symbol for the empress of China.

CRANE
The graceful crane symbolizes long life to the people in China.

Design an Emblem

The first emperor chose the dragon as his emblem. From then on, the dragon, particularly the yellow dragon, became the imperial symbol. Try to create your own emblem. It can be a real animal or a mythical one. It can be a plant or maybe something of your own creation. Think about what your emblem symbolizes.

DRAGON
In Chinese mythology, the dragon is wise and good. It has the head of a camel, antlers of a deer, ears of a cow, neck of a snake, eyes of a rabbit, and scales of a fish.

LOTUS
The lotus flower symbolizes purity.

SEW, A NEEDLE PULLING THREAD

Silk embroidery is an ancient art in China and is not for women only. Some embroidery is so elaborate, it can take five or six people several years to complete. Each style of silk embroidery takes images from the home region of the artist with designs of local flowers, trees, animals, and landscapes. Designs are often of traditional Chinese symbols, too, such as dragons, tigers, birds, chrysanthemums, lotus, bamboo, and landscapes of sampans (Chinese boats) and Chinese characters/words.

CHINESE EMBROIDERY

WHAT YOU NEED

Marker   #16 needle (for plastic canvas)
Yarn   #7 mesh plastic canvas (found at craft stores)

WHAT TO DO

1. With the marker, draw a design like a star or sunburst on the plastic canvas.

2. Thread the needle with about twelve inches of yarn. Tie a knot at the end of the longer end. Don't make the yarn too long or it will tangle.

3. Push needle up through a hole on the outline of the design (knot is on back). Skip three holes, then push your needle down into the fourth hole. Bring the needle up through the next hole. Continue along the lines of the design. When you get to the end of your yarn, tie a knot on the underside of the canvas, re-thread your needle and continue.

4. When you've completed the design, tie a knot on the underside and cut the extra length of yarn.

Say It!

Ci xiu (tze she-oh) is Mandarin for Chinese embroidery.

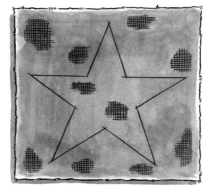

A Contrast in Music

Like just about everything in China, their music sounds very different from the music you listen to everyday. This is because traditional Chinese music uses a five-note scale whereas Western music uses an eight-note scale. In addition, the Chinese use musical instruments very different from the instruments used in the West. Let's take a look at a few of these instruments.

Xun (shoon) is one of the oldest instruments of China. An egg-shaped flute made from clay, its tone is haunting, yet simple. To play it, the musician blows into the top hole while placing fingers over the other holes.

Pipa (pee pah) is a stringed instrument. It's a type of lute but with a pear-shaped body. *Pi* means play forward. *Pa* means play backward. The musician plays the *pipa* by plucking the strings with long fingernails backwards and forwards.

Erhu (arh-hoo) is also a stringed instrument but, unlike the *pipa*, played with a bow, a little like a violin. Unlike the violin, however, the *erhu* is held upright. The *erhu* has a very long neck and only two strings. The *erhu* is also called a *huqin* (hoo-chin).

XUN

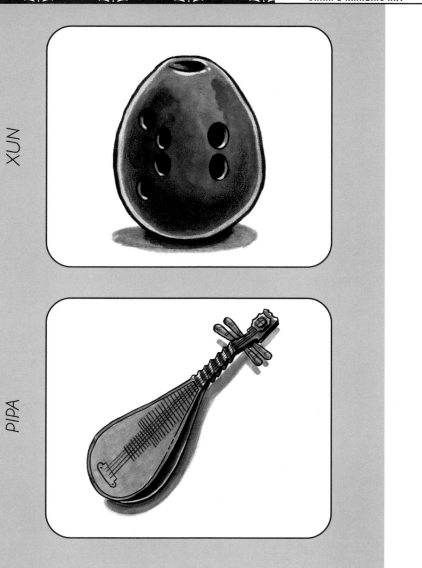

PIPA

THE ERHU AND BOW

MUSIC TO SOOTHE THE SOUL

During the Xia (2205–1776 BC), Shang (1766–1122 BC), and Zhou (1027–221 BC) dynasties, only royalty and court officials were allowed to even listen to music. Music was not thought of as a form of entertainment, but as a way of ridding the body of unrest. It wasn't until the Tang dynasty (AD 618–906) that dancing and singing were shared with the common people.

Try It!

Go to your local library and see if you can find a CD of traditional Chinese music. Listen to it. What makes it sound different from the music we are used to listening to? How does it make you feel?

CHINESE ACROBATICS

D o you ever think of acrobats as artists? Chinese acrobatics is a traditional performance art that dates back for more than 2,000 years. Acrobatic skills are handed down from one generation to another; and acrobats start training at a very young age, maybe even by six or seven years old. Becoming part of a Chinese acrobatic troupe takes many years of hard work and practice.

Chinese acrobatics include tumbling, magic, dance, juggling, and feats of balance. It also takes strength, flexibility, and agility. Jugglers use umbrellas, vases, plates, balls, chairs, poles, and ladders. Jugglers in these acts use almost any object and juggle them flawlessly. They use their hands *and* their feet, juggling objects alone or juggling them with a group of other performers.

Chinese acrobats integrate beautiful dance numbers into the show. In one act, a man and woman dance; and, using a long silk rope hanging from the rafters, they fly around the stage while the woman hangs upside down by her feet from the silk while holding on to the man as they glide through the air.

Acrobats twist their bodies into pretzel-like figures. While bending and flexing into many poses, acrobats balance items like glassware on their heads, hands, and feet. Skills in flexibility, strength, and balance are key.

Tumblers fly through the air as they somersault and leap across the stage. They may dive through small hoops, jump through the air, and then fold themselves so they fly through the hoop. Chinese acrobatics is truly an art as well as a skill.

Chinese acrobats

Juggling 2 balls

WHAT YOU NEED

2 balls, about the size of tennis balls

WHAT TO DO

1. Hold your arms naturally, bent at the elbows, and straight out. Hold one ball loosely in your right hand, don't grip tight.

2. Focus on two imaginary spots, at eye level, with each above your outstretched hands and six inches inside each outstretched hand. Toss the ball from your right hand up and to the left imaginary spot. When you "toss" the ball, try to toss from your palm. Let the ball fall into your left palm (Fig. 1).

3. With the ball in your left hand, toss the ball back up and to the imaginary spot above your right hand, again keeping your palm open somewhat. Let the ball fall into your right palm. Practice with 1 ball until you master the toss. Remember you are not "catching" the ball but letting it fall into your palm (Fig. 2).

4. Hold one ball in each hand. Toss one ball up and across just like you've been practicing. When this ball starts its downward arc, toss the second ball up and across. Each ball should cross over to the opposite hand. The rhythm is: throw, throw, catch, catch. Remember, juggling takes a lot of practice (Fig. 3).

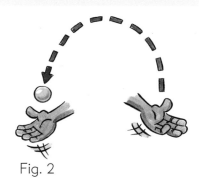

Fig. 1   Fig. 2

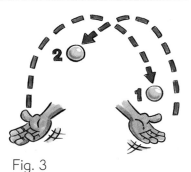

Fig. 3

More Than Chow Mein

Like most everything else in China, Chinese food has a history that goes back thousands of years. Each region of China has a distinctive cuisine because of the different climates of each area.

China also influenced neighboring countries with their cuisine. That's why you will find different versions of egg rolls in China, Vietnam, and Thailand.

Chinese immigrants even invented new dishes. In the 1880s, Chinese came to America to help build the railroads. Chop suey was created in America by those Chinese immigrants.

PONDER THIS

Ask your parents and grandparents what their favorite foods are. What are some of yours? Are they similar? Are there some traditional recipes that have been handed down from generation to generation? Have there been new ones created?

ANCIENT ICEBOXES

The ancient Chinese figured out that spoiled food not only tasted bad but could also make you sick. Starting in 1100 BC, the Chinese used ice to keep food fresh and cold. They also pickled and smoked meat and vegetables to preserve them and keep them from rotting.

FAMILY RECIPE BOOK

WHAT YOU NEED

Recipes from family members, including
    aunts and uncles and cousins
Paper
Pen

Markers, crayons, or paints
Card stock
3-hole punch
Yarn

WHAT TO DO

1. After you collect recipes from family members, write them down on paper.

2. Illustrate the recipes.

3. Put pages in whatever order you'd like (alphabetical, type of recipe, by age) and punch three holes along the left side (like a book).

4. Create the front and back cover with card stock. Give your family recipe book a title and write "Compiled by (your name)" on the front. Decorate the cover with markers.

5. Bind the book using yarn or string through the holes you punched. Tie securely.

Note: You can use a computer to type up the recipes and make multiple copies for family members. Or you can make copies of your hand-printed one on a copy machine. These would make great gifts for family members.

FOOD FROM NORTHERN CHINA

If you lived in northern China, perhaps in Beijing, you would eat noodles, dumplings, and steamed buns. Some of the dishes are Bird's Nest Soup, Peking Duck, and Moo-Shu Pork. By the way, Bird's Nest Soup is really made from a bird's nest! The cook uses the nest of a type of swift that builds its nests with a gummy saliva that hardens on cave walls and ceilings. Probably not something you would want to try!

KID-FRIENDLY DUMPLINGS

WHAT YOU NEED

1/2 pound ground beef
1/2 teaspoon salt

1 package wonton or gyoza skins
Soy sauce

WHAT TO DO

1. In a large bowl, combine ground beef and salt; mix well with a spoon.

2. Unwrap wonton or gyoza skins.

3. Drop a teaspoon of beef onto the center of one wonton skin (Fig. 1).

Fig. 1

4. Wash your hands well with lots of soap and water.

5. With your finger, moisten the edges of the skin and fold it over to shape a triangle or half circle, depending upon the shape of the skin you're using (Fig. 2). Press to seal edges (Fig. 3). Continue until you run out of meat or skins. Keep dumplings from touching each other or they'll stick together.

Fig. 2

6. Ask an adult to boil a large pot of water on the stove. Carefully drop half the dumplings into the boiling water and stir to keep from sticking. When water again comes to a boil, cook five minutes. Have an adult remove the cooked dumplings with a slotted spoon. Cook all of the dumplings.

7. Use soy sauce as a dipping sauce.

Fig. 3

FOOD FROM WESTERN CHINA

Children in western China, perhaps in Chengdu in Sichuan Province, eat the traditional hot and spicy dishes. In Chinese restaurants in the United States, these are often labeled Szechwan, Hunan, or Yunan. Hunan is the spiciest and uses fresh, hot chilies and lots of onions, garlic, ginger, pepper, peanuts, sesame seeds, and black beans.

Chili peppers at a spice market in Lijiang, Yunnan province

FOOD FROM EASTERN CHINA

Children in Shanghai eat lots of local fish, sweet potatoes, rice, corn, peaches, and chicken. Some of the traditional dishes from Eastern China include potstickers, salted pressed pork, and soup dumplings. These are the tiny dumplings filled with meat and soupy juice that explode with flavor in your mouth.

FOOD FROM SOUTHERN CHINA

If you lived in Guangzhou, or southern China, traditional food would include what is commonly known as Cantonese food. These are stir-fry dishes with no heavy sauces, lots of rice, and fresh vegetables with soy sauce and ginger. You might learn to love the frog's legs, pigeon, and snakes from this region! For snacks, there are plenty of locally grown citrus fruits.

ALL THE RICE IN CHINA

The Chinese began growing rice more than 6,000 years ago! Today, rice is so important that it provides daily nutrition for half the world's population. China is the world's top producer of rice; they grow over 40,000 *different* types of rice.

Rice is so important in China that it is a symbol for life. In fact, the word for rice in Chinese is the same as the word for food. Rice is served in some form at almost every meal and is considered part of the main course, not a side dish. The Chinese usually eat the long-grain variety of rice; sticky rice is used mainly for sweets.

SO WHAT'S A WOK?

Wok (in Cantonese) or *guo* (in Mandarin) means "cooking vessel" and is believed to have developed during the Han dynasty. The wok, a bowl-like pan, allows for good heat distribution and quick cooking.

WHAT'S RICE WITHOUT SOY SAUCE?

Soy sauce was invented during the Zhou dynasty and was originally a salty paste made from soybeans. It evolved into the liquid form we know and use today, made from pressed soybeans and roasted grain. Dark soy sauce is aged longer and is slightly thicker, while light soy sauce is saltier.

GROWING UNDERWATER

The Chinese were the first to grow rice in wet areas. Rice seed is first planted in a field of fertilized soil; but after about thirty days, workers transplant the seedlings to a water-filled rice paddy. Rice can grow underwater. After the mature rice is harvested, it is threshed to remove the bran layer that surrounds the grain. The bran layer is not removed in brown rice. There are different growing seasons for rice in the different regions of China, but most planting takes place in the spring and harvesting in late summer or early fall.

Try It!

The next time you're at the grocery store, count how many different types of rice you see. Probably not 40,000, but possibly more than one or two.

Planting rice in a flooded, terraced rice paddy

A RICE LEGEND

A very, very long time ago, a flood came and washed away the crops. There was nothing left for the people to eat. They prayed for a miracle. One day, a wild dog ran into town with yellow seeds stuck to his fur. The Chinese planted the seeds and they sprouted into rice. The people were saved from starvation.

Say It!

Mifan (mee fahn) is cooked rice in Mandarin.

Fan (fahn) means meal in Mandarin.

ALL THE TEA IN CHINA

The Chinese have been drinking tea for at least 4,000 years. Originally, tea was used to aid digestion. During the Three Kingdoms period (AD 220–589), Buddhist monks drank tea during meditation. Tea as a refreshment became widespread during the Tang dynasty (AD 618–907).

FOUR CHINESE TEAS

1. *Green Tea:* Fresh tea leaves are untreated before baking so they keep their natural color. Green tea is served in a white porcelain or pale green pottery pot with the cover off.

2. *Black Tea:* Tea leaves are fermented before baking. While we call this black tea, the Chinese call it *hong cha* or red tea. The Chinese believe black tea has warming properties and recommend it for drinking in the fall and winter.

3. *Wulong (Oolong) Tea:* Tea leaves are partially fermented. Wulong is often served in American Chinese restaurants.

4. *Scented Tea:* Tea leaves are mixed with various flower petals. Scented teas include jasmine, chrysanthemum, plum, and rose. These are served in celadon (pottery) or blue and white porcelain teapots with a cover.

Say It!

Cha (cha) means tea in Mandarin.

A tea plantation in Hangzhou, China

HAVE A
TEA TASTING

WHAT YOU NEED

Water
3 teacups or mugs
3 different flavors of tea in teabags
   (green tea, oolong tea, chamomile, fruit teas)

WHAT TO DO

1. With an adult's help, boil three cups of water.

2. In each cup, place one tea bag. Add hot water.

3. Let steep for about five minutes; remove tea bag. Allow tea to cool a little.

4. Smell the first tea. Does it smell sweet? Does it smell like fruit? Spice? Do you like the smell?

5. Take a sip of the first tea. Think about the flavor. Is it sweet? Bitter? What does it taste like? Do you like it?

6. Do the same for the rest of the teas. Do you have a favorite? Do you dislike any?

TEA FOR TWO OR MORE

The famous tea ceremonies of Japan first started in China during the Tang dynasty. The Japanese adapted and formalized it for their culture in the fifteenth century.

PONDER THIS

Take a look at Chinese teacups. They look very different from our Western teacups and mugs. Chinese teacups have no handles. If the teacup is too hot to pick up with your fingers, then it's definitely too hot to sip!

DIM SUM

Long ago, doctors thought that if people ate food with tea they would get very fat. Years ago, at day's end when weary travelers and workers looked for rest and refreshment, there were only tea houses and only tea was served. But since travelers and workers were hungry, tea houses became known for the snacks they served with tea. Those snacks became known as dim sum.

Today, eating dim sum is like eating brunch. Usually, instead of menus, waiters push carts around the restaurant loaded with baskets and plates of food. You can choose the foods you want from the carts.

HAVE SOME DIM SUM

There are many different kinds of food to eat at dim sum, but below are some popular items. These names are in Cantonese, not Mandarin, since dim sum originated in Guangzhou where Cantonese is spoken.

Char Siu Bao: Steamed buns with roast pork filling

Chee Cheong Fun: Rice pasta rolls, often flavored with shrimp and dipped in a sweet soy sauce mixture

Chun Juan (Mandarin): Crisp spring roll filled with vegetables and meat

Dan Taht: Sweet egg custard tart

Fung Jeow: Fried chicken feet (The Chinese consider this a delicious treat!)

Har Gow: Shrimp-filled steamed dumplings

Shu Mai: Pork-filled streamed dumplings

A DIM SUM LEGEND

During the Qing dynasty, the emperor liked to dress up like a commoner and mingle with the people. His servants would tag along, but they were told not to give away the emperor's true identity. One day while eating dim sum, the emperor was out dressed as a commoner, and he poured a cup of tea for his servant. The servant was so grateful he wanted to get down on his knees and bow to his emperor, but he knew that would give away his true identity. Instead, he tapped on the table to acknowledge the emperor's kindness. This tapping still means thank you.

Say It!

dim sum (dim some)—Cantonese

dian xin (dee ahn shin)—Mandarin for "dim sum." It means "a little bit of heart"

A LOTTA SNACKS

Since about the tenth century, over 2,000 different dim sum dishes have been created.

Steamed soup dumplings

MIND YOUR MANNERS

If you dine out for dim sum, there are customs you can follow. If your teapot is empty, turn the lid vertically on the pot to tell your server you need a refill. When someone fills your teacup, tap your finger in front of the teacup as a thank you.

LEARN MORE·LEARN MORE·LEARN MORE·LEARN MORE·LEARN MORE·LEARN MORE·LEARN MORE·LEARN MORE·

Read the picture book *Dim Sum for Everyone* by Grace Lin.

EATING WITH STICKS

Nobody really knows why chopsticks were invented; but the Chinese first used chopsticks about 5,000 years ago. Some stories say that people were so hungry, they couldn't wait for the food to cool off. Rather than burn their fingers, they broke off twigs to eat with. Another story says that as fuel became scarce, chefs chopped food into small pieces so they would cook faster. Since the food was already in bite-sized pieces, people no longer needed cutting utensils at the table and chopsticks became the main tableware by 400 BC. Around the same time, Confucius advised people not to use knives because it suggested violence. He preferred chopsticks because they reflected gentleness. By AD 500, chopsticks spread to Japan, Korea, and Vietnam.

Say It!

kauizi (kwai tze) means chopsticks in Mandarin. Literally translated it means "quick little fellows."

SOME THINGS TO DO . . .

1. Do pick up your rice bowl and hold it close to your mouth.
2. Do use the opposite end of your chopsticks to take food out of center serving platters if a separate serving utensil isn't offered.
3. Do set your chopsticks down on the table or chopstick rest provided in between use. (It's considered bad luck to rest your chopsticks parallel across your bowl.)
4. Do leave some food on your plate.
5. Do, do, do thank your host or hostess for a good meal!

SOME THINGS TO DON'T . . .

1. Don't suck on your chopsticks or leave them in your mouth.
2. Don't tap or drum your chopsticks on the table or plates. (Something beggars do.)
3. Don't point with your chopsticks.
4. Don't take the last bit of food from the serving platter. (Otherwise you imply to your host he/she didn't feed you enough.)
5. Don't stab your food with your chopsticks.
6. Don't stand your chopsticks upright in your bowl. (This is done during ceremonies for the dead. Definitely not appropriate for dining.)

Try It!

Once you have the hang of using chopsticks, see how many different kind of objects you can pick up.

MAKE MINE GOLD

Chopsticks can be made of almost any solid material such as ivory, jade, silver, bone, iron, bronze, and agate. Most chopsticks for home use are made of bamboo and wood. Chinese chopsticks are nine to ten inches (23–25 cm) long with a blunt end.

CHOPSTICK LESSON

WHAT YOU NEED

Pair of chopsticks
Piece of soft bread

WHAT TO DO

1. Pick up one chopstick. Rest it across the crook of your thumb and on your ring finger, holding it still with your middle finger.

2. Hold the second stick between your middle finger and your pointer finger, using your thumb to hold it steady. If this is too difficult, use your thumb and pointer finger (Fig. 1).

3. Move the upper stick in a pinching motion against the stationary lower stick. Try to pick up the piece of bread. This takes practice so don't give up (Fig. 2).

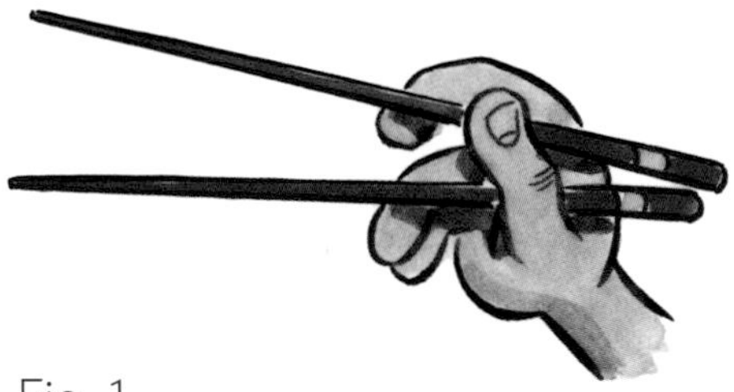

Fig. 1

Fig. 2

Some Disappearing Friends

China is home to many animal species, most of which you will see only in zoos. Unfortunately, because of pollution and loss of habitat, many of China's animals are in danger of extinction. Recently, the Chinese government has begun programs to protect most of these animals. Here are a few of the animals which are at critical risk.

THE GIANT PANDA

When you think of China, what animal comes to mind? Probably, the giant panda. These beautiful black and white creatures are considered national treasures of China. In 1957, the Chinese government understood they needed to act if they were going to save the panda from extinction. Panda hunting was officially banned in 1962 and worldwide efforts are underway to save the giant panda.

CONSERVATION STATUS -
Endangered. Approximately 1,600 pandas left in the wild.

LIKE A STICK OF BUTTER

When born, a panda cub weighs only about four ounces and is completely helpless.

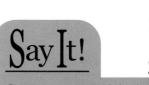

Say It!

Da xiongmao (dah she-ong-maoh) means giant panda.

ALL ABOUT THE GIANT PANDA

Common Name: Giant Panda
Scientific Name: *Alluropoda melanoleuca*
Range: Mountainous areas in central China (Sichuan, Shaanxi, & Gansu Provinces)
Habitat: Temperate forests
Diet: Bamboo leaves, stems, and shoots. An adult panda can eat 26–83 pounds of bamboo each day. That's like you eating 78–249 bananas every day!

MAKE A
PANDA MASK

WHAT YOU NEED

Coffee mug
Black construction paper
Pencil
Scissors

White, uncoated paper plate
Black marker or crayon
Craft stick
White glue or glue stick

WHAT TO DO

1. Use the coffee mug to trace a circle on black construction paper; cut it out.

2. Cut the circle in half. Set aside. These will be the giant panda's ears.

3. With an adult's help, hold the paper plate to your face and find where your eyes are. Make a mark with the pencil. Pull plate away from your face and have the adult cut out the eye holes.

4. On the back of the plate, draw oval patches around the eyeholes with a black marker. Color in. Draw a triangle for a nose and a black line for the mouth.

5. On each side of the top of the plate, glue on the half-circle ears. Glue the craft stick at the bottom so you can hold your giant panda mask over your face. Reinforce with tape if necessary.

WHAT ARE YOU TAKIN ABOUT?

The takin (rhymes with rockin') is a hoofed and horned animal that looks like a big shaggy mountain goat. Takin are losing their habitat to farming, mining, logging, and hunting. Chinese law now protects the takin, and breeding programs have been set up throughout the world.

Although adult male takins can weigh up to 880 pounds (400 kg) and adult females up to 550 pounds (250 kg), newborn takins weigh only between eleven and fifteen pounds (5–7 kg). Just minutes old, they can walk, run, and jump. Since takin are herd animals, even babies must move with the group to find food and escape predators.

Takin in the San Diego Zoo

CONSERVATION STATUS -
Endangered. Only an estimated several thousand are left in the wild.

ALL ABOUT THE TAKIN

Common name: Takin
Scientific name: *Budorcas taxicolor*
Range: mountain ranges in China and the eastern Himalayas
Habitat: temperate forests at elevations between 4,000 and 12,000 feet
Diet: plants

TAKIN vs WILD DOG GAME

WHAT YOU NEED

Large yard or area where you can safely run
At least 10 people

WHAT TO DO

Mark off playing area so there is a starting line and a finish line. Choose two people to be wild dogs. The rest of the group will be takin. Takin must hold their hands to their head like horns, putting thumbs to the sides of the head with pinkies pointing out.

1. Takin line up on one side of the playing area. This is the safe zone.

2. Wild dogs stand together in the center of the playing area.

3. Takin must run to the other side of the playing area (migrating to new grazing area) without being tagged by wild dogs. Wild dogs (hunting for food) try to tag migrating takin. Each time the takin run to other side equals one "season."

4. If a wild dog tags a takin, the takin becomes a wild dog. One wild dog can only tag one takin. By season two, if a wild dog is unable to tag a takin, wild dog becomes a takin (wild dog dies from starvation, as takin herd increase). Play for ten seasons.

Discussion: What happens when there are more wild dogs than takin? What happens to the wild dog pack when there aren't enough takin? Do takin ever completely disappear? Did that happen during your game? What does this tell you about the natural balance of predators and prey? Predators are animals that hunt other animals for food. Prey are animals that are hunted by other animals.

SOUTH CHINA TIGER

In China the tiger symbolizes strength. But today, the South China tiger may be extinct in the wild. It has not been spotted in over twenty years. In the 1950s tigers were considered pests and the country set about to destroy all. But in 1979 China banned the hunting of tigers, and by 2000 made saving them a priority. Unfortunately, there are no wild habitats left where the tigers can live. Because of this habitat loss, survival of the South China tiger in the wild is only a slim possibility.

ALL ABOUT THE SOUTH CHINA TIGER

Common name: South China Tiger
Scientific name: *Panthera tigris amoyensis*
Range: southeast China
Habitat: mountains, subtropical evergreen forests
Diet: carnivorous; eats mostly large mammals like deer and pig

Say It!

Lao hu (laow hoo) means tiger in Mandarin.

South China Tiger (Panthera tigris amoyensis) Nuremberg, Germany, Zoo

MAKE A
MAMMAL

WHAT YOU NEED

Index cards (or paper)
Pens or pencils
2 people
Selection of kitchen items,
    garden tools, or
    sports equipment

Suggestions: small spade,
spoon, nutcracker, tongs,
hammer, screwdriver, pliers,
soup ladle, rolling pin, raincoat,
(plastic) knife, tennis racket,
knee/elbow pads, helmet

WHAT TO DO

1. Make the habitat stack by writing each of the following words on an index card:
    arctic/snow, desert, mountains, rainforest, woods, edge of
    a river or stream

2. Make the food stack by writing each of the following words on an index card:
    seeds and nuts, other animals, fruit, plants, insects

3. Draw one card from the habitat stack and one card from the food stack.

4. Using the miscellaneous items you collected, make a mammal with adaptations for living in that habitat and eating that food item. One person makes the mammal, the second person becomes the mammal.

5. Make sure you have a reason for each item you use. Some examples: If the animal lives in the snow or the sand, it might have tennis rackets on its feet like snowshoes. If the animal eats other animals, it might have a plastic knife to cut its food with.

PONDER THIS

Why do you think animals live longer in captivity than in the wild? How do you feel about animals in captivity? Go to your local zoo and observe the animals. Are they in barred cages with concrete floors? Are the cages small? Or are they in larger exhibits that are created to look more like a natural habitat? Do they have room to run? Do they have a place to hide from the public eye? Why do you think zoos play an important role in the conservation of animals?

BOOKS FOR FURTHER READING

Bowler, Ann and Lak-Khee Tay-Audouard. *Adventures of the Treasure Fleet*. Rutland, Vermont: Tuttle Publishing, 2006.

Lin, Grace. *Dim Sum for Everyone*. Albuquerque, New Mexico: Dragonfly Books, 2003.

Jiang, Ji Li. *Red Scarf Girl*. New York: HarperCollins, 1998.

Cotterell, Arthur and Laura Buller. *Ancient China*. New York: DK Publishing, 2005.

Major, John S. *The Silk Route: 7,000 Miles of History*. New York: HarperTrophy, 1996.

O'Connor, Jane. *The Emperor's Silent Army: Terracotta Warriors of Ancient China*. New York: Viking, 2002.

Freedman, Russell. *Confucius: The Golden Rule*. New York: Arthur A. Levine Books, 2002.

Wexo, John Bonnett. *Giant Pandas*. Poway, California: Wildlife Education Ltd., 1989.

 About the Author

Debbi Michiko Florence is a California native; but she has called many places home including Mexico City, Mexico, and Shanghai, China. She is a former fifth-grade teacher, Associate Curator of Education for the Detroit Zoo, travel author, and children's author interviewer. Today, Debbi is a full-time children's author and writes from wherever home may be. You can always find her at http://www.debbimichikoflorence.com.

INDEX